Janet Connah

REFLECTIONS ON THE OUTSIDE WORLD AND WITHIN

A Collection of Poems

AUSTIN MACAULEY PUBLISHERS™

LONDON • CAMBRIDGE • NEW YORK • SHARJAH

The poem 'An Old Lullaby' on page 15 adapts text from the song 'Ma Curly-Headed Baby', popularised by Paul Robeson and composed by George H Clutsam (1866–1951).

A CIP catalogue record for this title is available from the British Library.

ISBN 9781528972093 (Paperback)
ISBN 9781398415515 (Hardback)
ISBN 9781398415522 (ePub e-book)

www.austinmacauley.com

First Published (2021)
Austin Macauley Publishers Ltd
25 Canada Square
Canary Wharf
London
E14 5LQ

DEDICATION

For my children Alison and Jonathan
and grandsons Sam, Ben, Charlie and Jack

PEOPLE

Odyssey of the Heart

I. Enchantment

You stole a glance at me
From eyes of azure blue
Like the flash of sunlight on a halcyon sea
That look
Lighting my heart and senses
With a first awakening of love.

Soon, enchanted, I was captive in your sway
Our love, afire, flaming each golden day
With joy in our togetherness, a passion shared
You and I, desiring no one, nothing more, who could have dared
To try and break the spell of such happiness?

II. Disillusionment

I saw you look at her in that way you have
With that same glance which entranced me from the first.
We have so often quarrelled recently
Over this and that – small things
Which did not really matter – or so it seemed
My love remains still strong, invincible.
But you no longer share my dreams
And spent passion has replaced my mystery
Tiring of the familiar, you may leave me.

III. Finale

I only walked this way so if by chance, I might see you
In the place where oft we strolled together
Arm in arm along the summer lane
I hoped that you too might be there
And if you caught a glimpse of me
You would stop and say hello for old time's sake
Our one last meeting might ease the heart break
Yet I stand alone in the silent lane
Empty now but for the drift of fallen leaves
Blown by the first winds of autumn
I feel their chill and sadly turn away
Knowing I will never again walk this way.

IV. Restoration

Thoughts of you blow in
Across the waste lands of a broken heart
As the tumble weed on a dust filled plain
Unbidden and unwanted.

Through empty, endless days and weeks
I bear the pain of our lost love
Remembering your warmth and laughter
The grace of your presence.

Today a stranger spoke to me
With a smile that shone into my soul
As it lit the darkness within my heart
I saw at last the vision of a new beginning
And suddenly, there among the tumble weed
Sprang a small shoot of vibrant green.

Summer

She steals uninvited through my open window
Her glance, a gleam of gold, lightens the dimness of the room
As it gilds my face, gentle and warm
I am soothed as if by a southern breeze
Her perfume is floral scented from the garden beyond
Her dress, a rainbow of colour – jewel green, sky blue, scarlet and the
  purest white
Her voice, the sound of bird song, the hum of bees, the sway of leaf and
  the ripple of water,
I sit silent as if mesmerised by her lustrous beauty
And then I welcome her with joy
For she is summer!

The Ladies of the Buffet Bar

The ladies of the buffet bar rise every morning at three
For the early morning shift when they prepare coffee, tea
And a welcome for the weary rail commuters, faces, tired and grey,
With tickets for the early train which starts their working day.
But first a warming drink in the buffet served deftly with a smile
By the ladies at the counter, Mary and her partner, Di
Both middle aged, they too are tired and need to fortify themselves.
Mary, rising in the early dark at home, drinks three cups of tea
Before she can come round and go and see
If the cat is there waiting to be let in.
Di slowly savours her one cigarette and a cup of tea
Before she dons her uniform, it helps her feel alive
To face another working day – the buffet opens at five.
They are quick and slick with service, no fumbling with the till
Countless cups of tea and Barista coffee, biscuits, papers,
A smile as they give you the bill
Mary and Di, the unsung heroines of a working week
And like so many of their ilk, they do not seek
Praise or recognition but it is the workers such as they
Who smooth the path of thousands on many a working day.

A Boy Named Brown

Do you recall a boy named Brown?
He was in our third-year class quite some years ago.
His name well suited him – Brown
Light brown hair and hazel eyes, of medium height
In class, he had quietly gained average marks,
Reasonably sporty I suppose, but seemingly unremarkable
His was a steady presence among his livelier peers
Well I saw him again the other day
Just by chance at the bus stop in the town
There he stood, tall and handsome – Brown
He spoke and welcomed me with a radiant smile
It was as if since those early days of youth
A transformation had wakened a vibrant spirit
He is studying engineering now, a good degree
In that brief, glad meeting it was as if l saw
The shining path his life would take
And for a fleeting moment as we parted I was saddened
That I could not share that way.

An Old Lullaby

As my mother lay ill and dying
I sang to her a lullaby
As old and timeless as the sky
Lulla, Lulla, Lullaby
It was the same song she sang to me
When as a small child I lay
Sleepless, ill or full of fears,
So I sang to her through my tears
Lulla, Lulla, Lullaby,
I hoped she heard the words and the soft tune
Gave her comfort. Its simple verse, of stars and moon
"Oh Lulla, Lulla, Lulla, lulla-by-by
Do you want the stars to play with?
The moon to run away with?
They will come if you don't cry."
These words of solace by me were chosen
Though both mind and heart by grief were frozen.

PLACES

This Place

This place is where the king cups grew
In a profusion of gold by the old mill stream
This place is where drifts of bluebells lay
In a blue haze beneath the woodland fringe
This place is the meadow beyond clothed in clover, daisy and buttercup
And summer grasses blowing in the wind.
This place is where we laughed and played as children
Formed bonds for life with carefree games
This place, our place, abides forever
For though those precious days and fields are now long gone
We are together still
Shared memories of them and you live on.

The Last Shepherd – Portuguese Heritage

There is a sweet chiming of neck bells as the sheep pass
Amid the scent of wild herbs in the sun warmed pasture
They are remnants of a bygone age this flock
An ancient breed, long horned, long limbed
They meander by, slowly grazing.
Their guardian, an old dog, is wolfhound bred, his stature long and lean.
Their master too, is elderly, stooped and worn.
The path they tread is an age-old route
Through farmland abandoned long ago
Its stone aqueducts remain intact
Amid the groves of stunted olive trees and herbage.
 Come noon day heat, the group will rest in shade,
For these are southern climes
There sheep, man and dog, are joined by another flock
A flight of white plumed egrets flutter in
Theirs is a pastoral scene unchanged through centuries
But there, beyond the headland, lie the walls of new built villas
Set amid green, pristine lawns and the gleam of concrete roads.
For now, this last shepherd and his flock remain,
They are symbols of a lost heritage.

Pennine Landscape

I evolved from you
Your harsh, cold clime has shaped my form.
My bleak boulders and black tarns
Reflect the brooding darkness of your northern skies
My sparse grasslands and leaning furze
Bend to the power of your cruel winds.
Scattered farmsteads huddle into hillsides
Stone walls, slate roofs, in seeming harmony
With this terrain of greyness and muted colour
It is no place for soft comfort.

Yet I have beauty too
My land is clean cut – untamed,
Its hills sharp defined against the skyline
There is a visual wonder in the wild rain squalls.
Blown and swept in sudden fury across my fells
In the cold mists which shift and blur the looming crags.

In summer sunlight and shadow dance across my moors
Their shifting visions of shape and movement
Reflect the cloud patterns of the sky
In a swirling kaleidoscope display
Of shade and brightness.

In winter when snow smoothes the barren, sharpness of my ridges
Softens the sunless depths of my ravines
I flaunt a white, boundless cloak of sparkling light
I bathe in fragile beauty, a transient delight.

CHILDREN

The Supermarket Queue

We hate the supermarket queue
When people stand too close to you,
And tut if there is some delay
Or think you take too long to pay

We hate the supermarket queue
When people just in front of you
Have a packet of 'wotsits' with no price
You must be patient and try to be nice
But the minutes tick by as staff try to find out
You cannot frown but you want to shout

We hate the supermarket queue
We could be through in a minute or two
If we could find an empty till
It would not take long to pay our bill
And Dad's at home and wants his tea
And we children do not want to be
Here, waiting…
Mum, it really is down to you.
We hate the supermarket queue.
The self-serve tills are all taken too.

Dear children please do not whine
And no, I don't want to shop on line.
At last, we are in luck – Here's an empty aisle.
Say hello to the till lady and give her a smile
Help me load up the shopping. Don't give any cheek
It's over at last 'til we are here again next week.

The Battle of the iPad

Can I have the iPad Dad?

Go and ask your mother

Can I have the iPad Dad?

Just go and play with your little brother

Please can I have the iPad Dad?
Say yes and I won't be bad
Ever again!

Son, you know the iPad rule
Not on week nights because of school
It really is your mother who has the say
So please I'm reading, go away

But I have already asked her Dad
She just said "no" and then got mad
So please can I have the iPad, Dad?

Dustbins and Dragons

Like a huge yellow dragon, it roars into the close
Then swirling with a hiss of brakes it stops
And opens its cavernous mouth to swallow up
The offerings of the day,
It grabs and tips the lines of helpless dustbins
Their fillings, household left overs and bags of this and that
Are crushed into nothingness by its huge steel jaws
It makes a fearful sound.
Then with another roar, it is gone down the lane
The dustbin lorry and its crew of men.
Next week, when hungry, it will come again
It really scares my little brother
As it nears the house, he clings to mother
All the grown-ups say it's just a wagon
But take a peep through the eyes of a child
You too would see a fearsome dragon.

The School Run

Henry, we'll be late for school
Are you up yet?
"No!"
Well, my son, you know the rule
No iPad, football or swimming pool
If we are late again
So it's down to you
Do please hurry and get dressed
Every morning I get stressed
I have to get to work on time
Just for once please toe the line
"Shan't I'm tired!"
Henry I am shouting up the stair
Are you washed yet? Your breakfast's here
I cannot make myself more clear
I simply cannot have this any more
So I am going – Mum slams the door
"Muuum, Mummee! – "Yes Henry?"
"I am coming now so please will you wait?
It's just the rushing I really hate,
You can drop me off by the school gate."
Big sigh from Mum – Here we go again!

GENERAL

The Old Ways

They call them the old ways
The drovers' tracks, the bridle paths
The byways used by country folk
Treading the unmarked trails
Twixt village, farm and homestead
Our ancestors, long dead.

Yet some remain still, the old ways
Stray alone from a roadside verge
Into the depths of the valley beyond
Enter the gloom of an ancient woodland,
Silent and dim, its trees cluster and brood
To shut the sunlight from dark forest paths.
Suddenly the senses are alerted with a faint unease
By the sudden creak of a windswept bough,
The shrill screech of a disturbed bird,
The patter of leaf fall,
Walk briskly then from the wood to the sun warmed heath
Leave the shadows, sounds and memories undisturbed
For those were the old ways.

Wifely Conversation by a Holiday Poolside

"They say it's really nice at home, it's always been the way
It forecast 35 degrees here tomorrow
We won't cope by mid-day!
Despite the towels on sun beds ban
All the best shady spots are always gone,
Taken by the family of that awful looking man
Do try and mention it to him if you think you can
I wonder what's on the dinner menu, did you have a look?
I think I'll go in soon and finish off my book
What about that friendly couple next to us at dinner?
I find them somewhat boring. Her looks are not a winner!
The pool looks so inviting, why don't you take a dip?
Oh and can you remember to book us seats for the coach trip?
Well that's enough for one day, we'll look forward to tonight
Will that lady in the purple frock be there? She really looks a fright!
Make sure we get lounge seats at the very back, I cannot stand
   much noise
I think the flamenco dancers are the best, they always have such poise
Do go early in the morning to get our daily paper
They, like the sun beds, were all gone today – it really is a caper
Could you pop down to the shop and get some pills for Jill?
She isn't looking well at all– I told you she'd be ill
Oh well, only three more days to go, I hope the cat's alright
And our neighbour has remembered to let him out each night
Aren't we having a lovely time? I'm really glad we came
It's just I hate the airport and boarding that enormous plane
I really object to being herded just like sheep
Shuffling along the roped-off lanes is like walking in one's sleep
Then having to take our shoes off, pile trays high with all our gear
But like you, I can't wait to plan our time away next year!"

Kitchen Mugs

The kitchen mugs don't know the drill
They range along the window sill
Laze on the desk and bedside table
Sometimes for a day or two.
Oh how I wish that they were able
To take themselves back to the kitchen sink
Instead of making me have to think
Now where are they?
There's young Sam's mug with spots and stripe;
Mum's is floral with a China sheen
And Dad's gardening mug, a present from Aunty Jean
Then there's a hand painted matching pair
Who only appear when visitors are there
And lined along the cupboard back
An aged group of mugs with chip and crack,
At least they might see some light of day
Far more than the best China cups can say
Sitting on the display shelves, all lonely and neat
They hope in vain to appear
At an afternoon's tea treat.

In the Night

Fox in the night
I hear the sharp shriek of your bark
Primeval sounding from the wood beyond
You flicker, flame red in the darkness
As you prowl and hunt

Owl in the night
Beauteous ghost in silent, deadly flight
Silk, sleek preened feathers on outstretched wing
I hear your short screech call across the frosted meadow
Then silence as you swoop to make your kill

Cat in the night
I hear you yowl and spit
Prowling the dew damp darkness of urban paths
Stalking soft pawed along the garden hedgerows
Hunting the hapless birds and mice.

Moon in the night
A silent, scimitar shape shines like a silver blade
Piercing the scudding clouds
Or rounded in benign, soft fullness
Glows golden with ethereal light.

Wind in the night
I hear your powerful howl and roar
As you rattle doors and windows
Swirl the trees, whip and tear leaf and branch
Beat hail against the roofs and shutters
Or softly moan as if in pain.

With daylight comes the morning sun
The sweet chorus of birds
The road hum of early traffic
Familiar sounds herald the new day
Things of the night quite banished away.

Lost Letters

They tumble through my letter box offers in the mail
Discount at the big-name stores with details of their sale
Letters from a charity asking for donations
Banks and financiers offering loan sensations
Letters, letters every day oh will they ever end
My email box too is full of them from companies pressing 'send'.

But where have all the letters gone from people we once knew
Love letters from sweethearts promising to be true
Sealed with 'SWALK' and 'BOLTOP',* inked messages of love
Written on scented note paper with drawings of a dove
And letters from the family, scattered far and wide
"Our Jimmy is doing well at school but our little dog has died."

Letters then which filled us with sadness or with joy
"We are so pleased to tell you that we have a baby boy
There's a picture of him enclosed within
He is lovely. Do you think he has his grandad's chin?"
But now computer screens show pictures of those we hold most dear
It's instant messaging on smart phones, pads, tablets and all that gear.

I keep my family letters as a memento of those lost days
When life was very different with the old familiar ways
Those letters are a history of life in all the years gone by
Communications good and bad, which made us laugh or cry
I have a bundle of letters tied with ribbon blue
To me they are the most precious because they came from you.

---

* 'Sealed With A Loving Kiss' and 'Better On Lips Than On Paper', respectively.

ABOUT THE AUTHOR

Educated at Newton-le-Willows Grammar school and
St. John's College, Manchester, the author is a former
journalist. She joined her home town local newspaper as a
junior reporter eventually becoming its news editor. She
went on to work as the press officer of a local authority
before joining the government information service where
she was employed in regional and national press offices.
In her later career she worked on media campaigns in the
United Kingdom and Europe. She is married with two
children and four grandsons.